# The Oxford Piano Method

## 20 Prehistoric Pieces and Puzzles

### by

# Pauline Hall and Paul Drayton

MUSIC DEPARTMENT

**OXFORD**

UNIVERSITY PRESS

# OXFORD
### UNIVERSITY PRESS

Great Clarendon Street, Oxford OX2 6DP, England
198 Madison Avenue, New York, NY10016, USA

Oxford University Press is a department of the University of Oxford.
It furthers the University's aim of excellence in research, scholarship,
and education by publishing worldwide in

Oxford  New York

Auckland  Bangkok  Buenos Aires  Cape Town  Chennai
Dar es Salaam  Delhi  Hong Kong  Istanbul  Karachi  Kolkata
Kuala Lumpur  Madrid  Melbourne  Mexico City  Mumbai  Nairobi
São Paulo  Shanghai  Taipei  Tokyo  Toronto

Oxford is a registered trade mark of Oxford University Press
in the UK and in certain other countries

19

ISBN 0-19-372766-8

Music and text origination by
Seton Music Graphics Ltd., Ireland

Printed in Great Britain by
Halstan & Co. Ltd., Amersham, Bucks

Illustrated by Peet Ellison

# Contents

# Stegosaurus stomp

This must sound loud but you don't need to hit the keys—just use firm fingers and let your arm feel heavy. It's a good idea to practise the right-hand chords first.

# Monstersearch

In the square below you will find the names of seven prehistoric monsters. There are also eleven things that they might do. How many can you find? (To make it a bit easier, the words only go across and down, not diagonally.)

| T | R | O | T | A | B | D | F | H | J | P | D |
| P | V | P | Y | L | I | R | O | M | P | L | I |
| H | C | T | R | L | F | I | G | H | T | E | P |
| S | T | E | G | O | S | A | U | R | U | S | L |
| A | Z | R | M | S | N | D | B | S | G | I | O |
| M | P | O | Q | A | C | I | R | T | L | O | D |
| B | L | D | R | U | H | N | O | O | I | S | O |
| L | A | A | O | R | E | O | W | M | D | A | C |
| E | Y | C | A | U | W | S | S | P | E | U | U |
| U | N | T | R | S | G | A | E | H | I | R | S |
| A | C | Y | D | F | M | U | N | C | H | J | K |
| V | E | L | O | C | I | R | A | P | T | O | R |

# Ambling Allosaurus

This is a happy, carefree sort of piece. There's no hurry—Allosaurus is strolling along and has time to look around and hum a little tune.

What is the key signature of F major?

What is the sharp in the key of G?

How would you play this note?

How many counts?

What does this sign mean?

# Fossilized footprints

Track the dinosaur to its lair by following its footprints. Answer the questions as you go along.

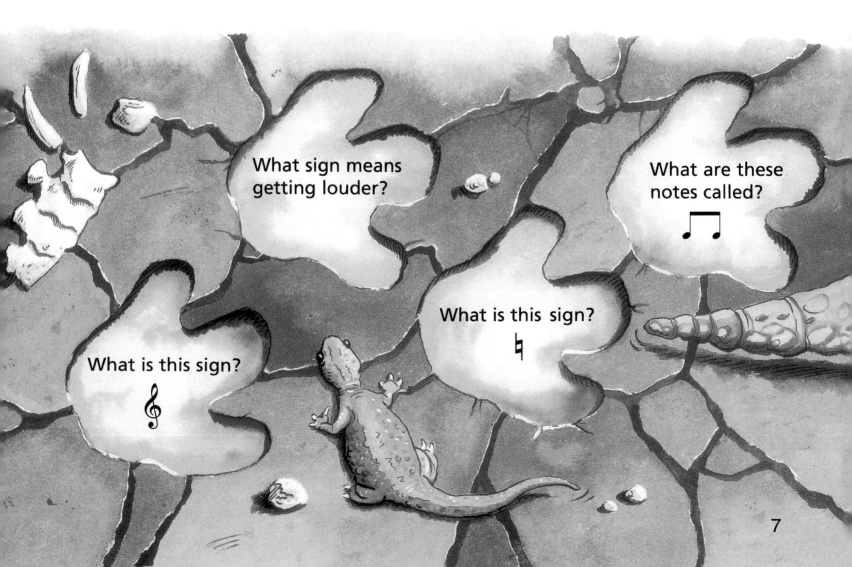

# Browsing Brontosaurus

The Brontosaurus here is eating quietly, moving slowly along as it munches. It's a good idea to learn the left-hand pattern in bars one and two first—it keeps reappearing!

**Chewing contentedly**

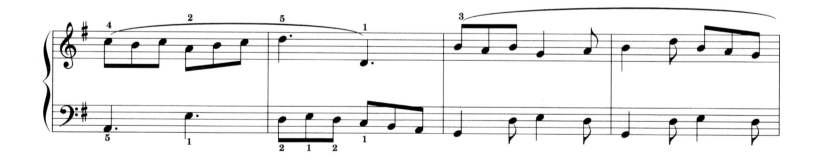

# A reminder about note values

This is just a sort of arithmetic.

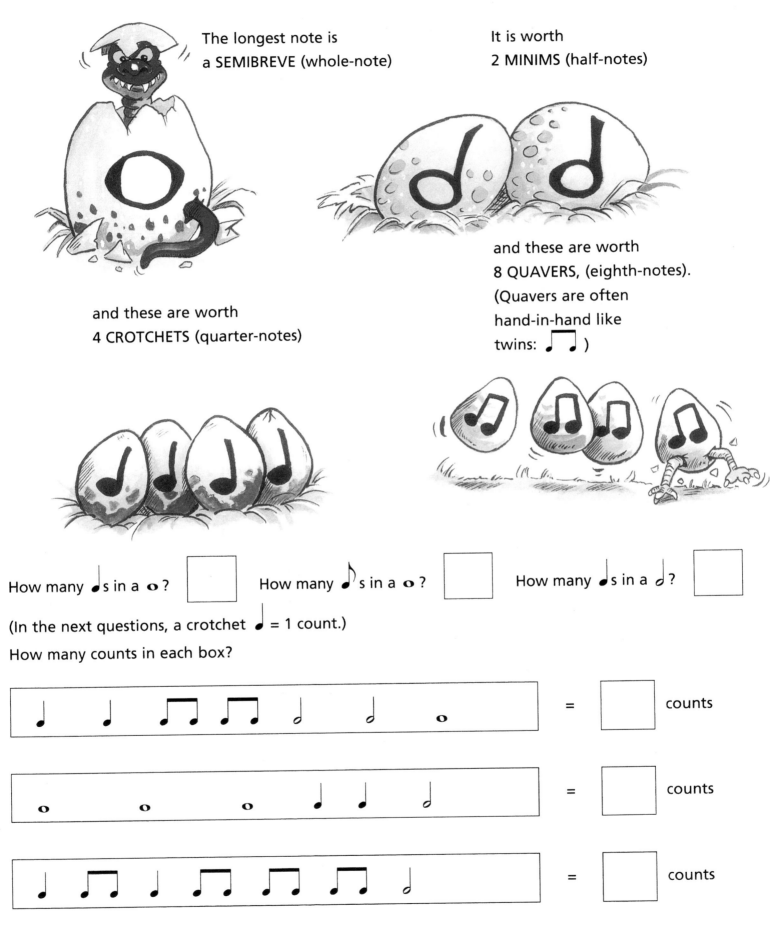

The longest note is
a SEMIBREVE (whole-note)

It is worth
2 MINIMS (half-notes)

and these are worth
4 CROTCHETS (quarter-notes)

and these are worth
8 QUAVERS, (eighth-notes).
(Quavers are often
hand-in-hand like
twins: ♫ )

How many ♩s in a 𝅝?  [ ]    How many ♪s in a 𝅝?  [ ]    How many ♪s in a ♩?  [ ]

(In the next questions, a crotchet ♩ = 1 count.)

How many counts in each box?

♩  ♩  ♫  ♫  ♩  𝅗𝅥  𝅗𝅥  𝅝   =  [ ]  counts

𝅝  𝅝  𝅝  ♩  ♩  𝅗𝅥   =  [ ]  counts

♩  ♫  ♩  ♫  ♫  ♫  𝅗𝅥   =  [ ]  counts

9

# Playful Plesiosaurs

These Plesiosaurs are really splashing about. Every so often one pops up from behind a wave to give the others a fright. Don't forget, the notes with an > above them should be played with a BIG accent.

**Frisky (a bit *too* frisky!)**

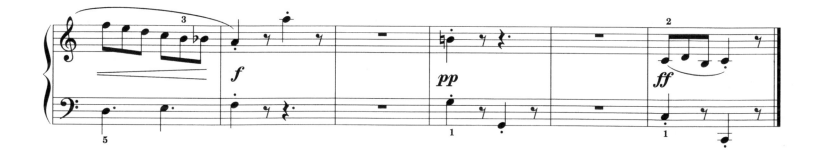

# Sharps and flats

Here's your chance to become an expert on sharps and flats. People (but not you) often make the mistake of drawing the sharp and flat signs in the wrong place. Sharps sit with their cross-bars on each side of the line or space they belong to.

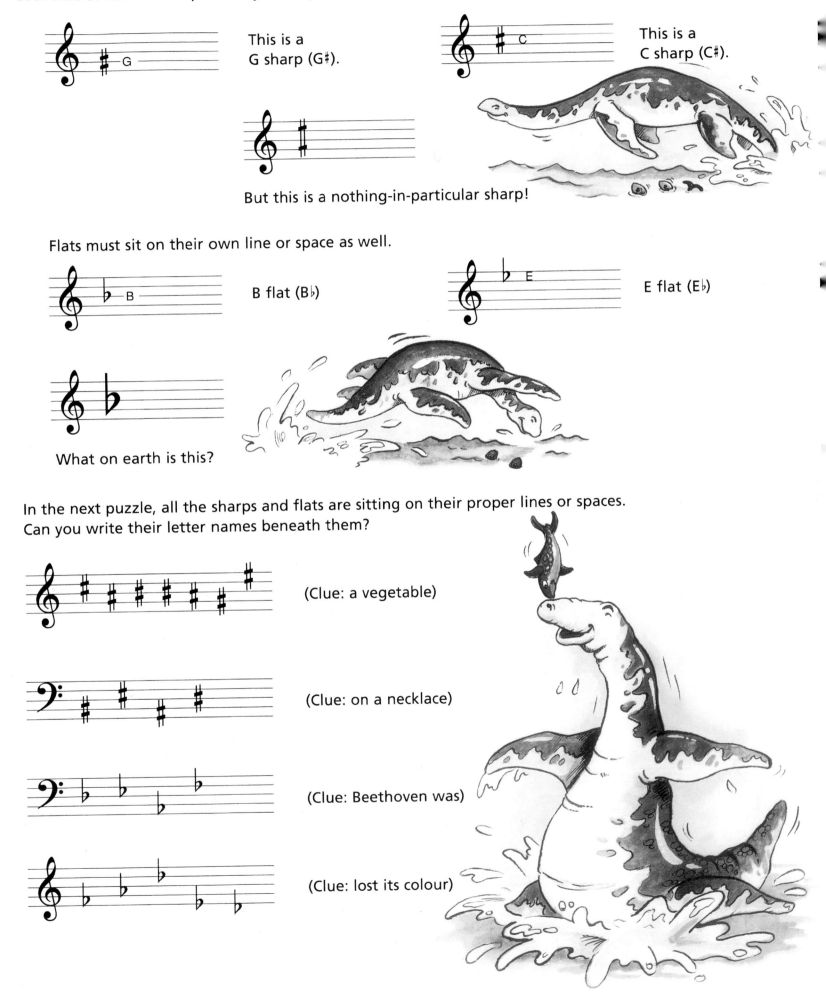

This is a G sharp (G♯).

This is a C sharp (C♯).

But this is a nothing-in-particular sharp!

Flats must sit on their own line or space as well.

B flat (B♭)

E flat (E♭)

What on earth is this?

In the next puzzle, all the sharps and flats are sitting on their proper lines or spaces. Can you write their letter names beneath them?

(Clue: a vegetable)

(Clue: on a necklace)

(Clue: Beethoven was)

(Clue: lost its colour)

# Triceratops trot

**Brisk and cheerful**

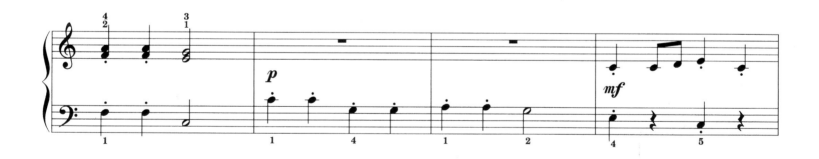

# Depths and heights

You are a deep-sea diver, and your job is to locate valuable treasure, lying deep below the surface of Loch Ness. All the pieces of treasure are notes on leger lines. When you have found them, take them to the surface and write their letter-names in the submarine's portholes. Beware of the Loch Ness monster!

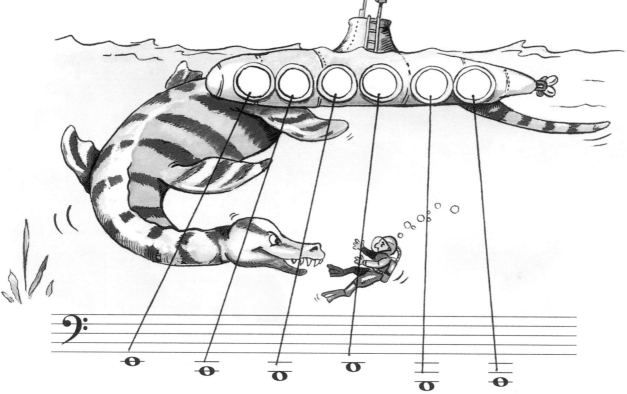

Time for a change of job now:

As an astronaut, you must retrieve stray pieces of satellite, floating high in space. They are notes on leger lines too. Locate them and send them down to the space station—but be careful!

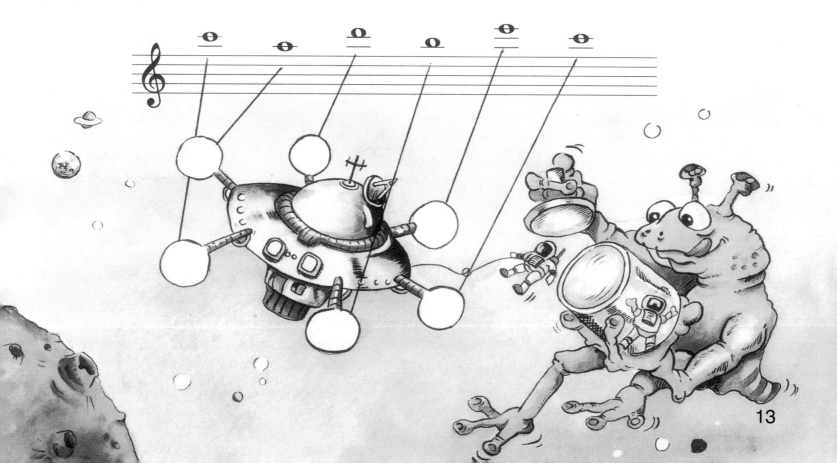

# The very vicious Velociraptor

This piece must sound really nasty.

**Very fast and snappy**

$\frac{2}{2}$ means that you count 2 beats in a bar, but each beat is a minim (half-note). Before you can play this piece fast you'll need to practise it slowly, counting 4 crotchets (quarter-notes) in a bar.

# The Scaleosaurus

This is a Scaleosaurus. Hidden amongst its scales are 5 musical scales, which go from left to right. There are 8 notes in each scale, and the notes are all on touching scales.

The scales are:

C major

G major

F major

D major

A harmonic minor

When you have found one, draw a line linking up its notes. (You might use a different-coloured line for each scale.) Then play each one, first with your right hand, then with your left.

On the monster's tail is a CHROMATIC scale. Can you play it? Use your 3rd finger on all black keys.

# Never vex a Tyrannosaurus Rex!

Tyrannosaurus Rex is quite alright if left alone, but if teased it can be terrifying. The piece gets gradually louder and louder right up to the end—what do you think happens in the last bar? Try playing the left-hand part an octave lower for a real dinosaur growl!

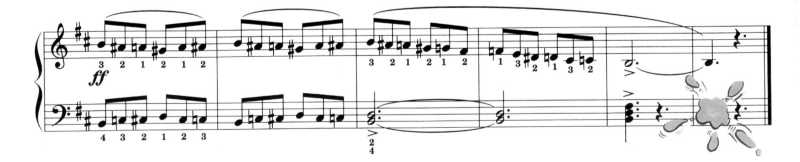

Lowest three notes
on piano (A, A♯, B)

# Make up a monsterpiece

First, decide what kind of monster you're composing about. Is it huge and heavy with big feet? Is it slithery and crawly? Or perhaps it's fluttery and squawky?

You'll need to play low down in the bass—at least one octave below middle C for your right hand, and two octaves below (or even three) for your left hand.

You might try something like this:

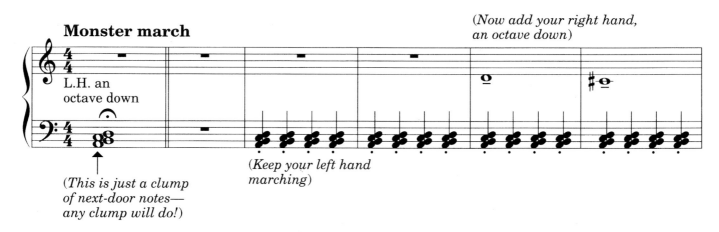

Making up music as you go along is called IMPROVISING. You'll get better at it as you experiment with different sounds. Try another monsterpiece, but this time make it different.

# Diplodocus drag

This piece must crawl along very slowly and smoothly—there are no staccato notes at all.

**Slowly slithering**

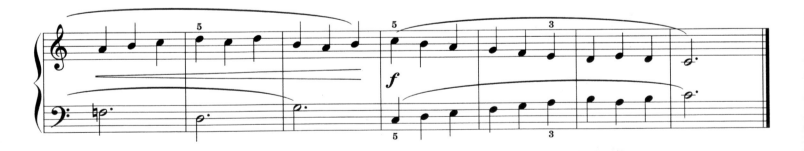

# Games for two to play

Try playing these games with your teacher or a friend. They're all on the white notes of the piano.

## Up or down

*Player 1* plays a note and then plays the note next-door to it, either up or down.
*Player 2* (who mustn't look at the keyboard) guesses the direction and says 'up' or 'down'.

After 4 turns the players change places and the game goes on to . . .

## Twos or threes

From one white note to the next is called a SECOND.

From one white note to the next but one is called a THIRD.

Before you begin the game, play the following and listen carefully to the difference.

Player 1 plays two notes one after the other.
*Player 2* guesses whether the notes were a 2nd or a 3rd apart.

After 4 turns change places, and finally . . .

## Find the fourths

A FOURTH has 2 notes between the 2 outside ones.

Listen to this.

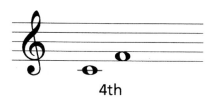

*Player 1* plays either a 2nd, a 3rd, or a 4th.
*Player 2* guesses.

You have 4 turns each.

# Pterodactyl glide

This Pterodactyl seems to be trying out a sort of flying waltz. Look out for the little slurs between pairs of notes in the right hand, and make the second note in each one a light staccato.

After many attempts, and a lot of flapping around, the Pterodactyl is finally airborne!

## A tip from two Pterodactyls

In music, notes which sit BELOW the third line have their tails going UP.

Notes which sit ABOVE the third line have their tails going DOWN.

Notes on the middle line can have their tails either way.

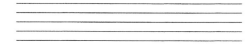

Add a few more notes to the stave opposite. Take care with their tails!

# Jurassic jamboree

At the end of another long, hot, prehistoric day, the dinosaurs gather together for a huge and noisy party. Play this piece with good rhythm and plenty of energy to get the dinosaurs really dancing!

# Musical puzzles

How many musical words can you find? They go across, down, and diagonally, and some read backwards. When you find a word, write it down in the box.

| S | O | N | A | I | P | S | S | A | B |
|---|---|---|---|---|---|---|---|---|---|
| T | Q | R | V | L | M | I | N | I | M |
| A | L | U | X | M | E | U | B | E | C |
| C | F | L | A | T | D | G | L | E | M |
| C | R | G | H | V | I | B | A | K | I |
| A | M | N | O | T | E | J | L | T | N |
| T | S | H | A | R | P | R | U | V | O |
| O | N | O | T | P | S | T | B | A | R |
| D | R | A | O | B | Y | E | K | W | X |

## Snap!

There are six symbols used in the cards below:

Can you find two cards that contain the same signs?

(These aren't necessarily in the same order.)